Abigail Adams

First Lady

Tamara Orr Staats

Boston, Massachusetts
Chandler, Arizona
Glenview, Illinois
Upper Saddle River, New Jersey

Illustrations

Opener, 1, 2, 4, 5, 6, 10, 12, 14 Norbert Sipos.

Photographs

Every effort has been made to secure permission and provide appropriate credit for photographic material.
The publisher deeply regrets any omission and pledges to correct errors called to its attention in subsequent editions.

Unless otherwise acknowledged, all photographs are the property of Pearson Education, Inc.

Photo locators denoted as follows: Top (T), Center (C), Bottom (B), Left (L), Right (R), Background (Bkgd)

3 Prints and Photographs Division, LC-DIG-ppmsca-15705/Library of Congress; 7 Detroit Publishing Company Photograph
Collection, Prints and Photographs Division, LC-D4-17010/Library of Congress; 8 Prints and Photographs Division,
LC-USZC4-1583/Library of Congress; 9 Prints and Photographs Division, LC-USZC2-2243/Library of Congress; 11 Prints
and Photographs Division, LC-USZC4-4970/Library of Congress; 13 Prints and Photographs Division, LC-USZC2-2645/
Library of Congress; 15 Prints and Photographs Division, LC-USZ62-10016/Library of Congress.

ISBN-13: 978-0-328-67638-5
ISBN-10:   0-328-67638-1

9 10 11 V0SI 17 16 15

A Remarkable Woman

Abigail Adams lived at a time when women had few choices. In the 1700s most women did not go to school. They could not vote. If they were married, they could not own property. Only men had a say in government.

Abigail Adams was one woman who did not let these problems stop her. Despite the lack of choices facing women, she had a lot of **influence**.

John Adams

Like most young girls of her time, Abigail Adams did not go to school. She was taught at home. Still, she became very well educated. She helped shape history by advising her husband, John Adams. He was the second president of the United States.

Growing Up

Abigail Adams was born Abigail Smith on November 11, 1744, in Weymouth, Massachusetts. Her father, William Smith, was the town minister. He had a large library. He wanted his four children to share his love of learning, even his daughters. He encouraged them to read as much as possible.

Education

Abigail Smith was taught to read and write by her mother. She loved to read, and tried to learn as much as she could. But all her life, she was embarrassed by her poor spelling and grammar. She wished she could have gone to school. She felt it was very unfair that girls were not given the same education as boys.

John Adams

In 1762, Abigail Smith met a young lawyer named John Adams. They fell in love. The two lived only five miles from each other and saw each other often. They also wrote many letters to each other.

John Adams was born in this house on October 30, 1735.

Marriage

John and Abigail Adams were married on October 25, 1764. They were partners for 54 years.

The couple settled at John Adams's farm in Braintree, Massachusetts. John Adams became a very important leader in the American **colonies**, which were ruled by Great Britain. Because of his work, the two were often apart. During this time, they wrote each other hundreds of letters.

Colonists protested against British taxes.

Boston and Philadelphia

In 1768, John and Abigail Adams moved to Boston. He needed to be close to his work. Abigail Adams loved the busy city life. She had lots of interesting visitors and plenty to talk about.

The American colonists and the British were not getting along. Some Americans were calling for **independence**, or to be free of British rule.

John Adams was sent to Philadelphia as a **delegate** to the Continental Congress. One goal of the Congress was to discuss independence.

Like her husband, Abigail Adams supported independence. She felt it was John Adams's duty to serve in the Congress. But she missed him terribly.

In 1775, war broke out between the colonists and the British. It was called the American Revolution.

John Adams (at right) was on a committee to write the Declaration of Independence.

Managing the Farm

While John Adams was away, Abigail Adams moved back to the farm in Braintree. It was now up to her to run the farm. She tended the crops and managed the workers. She milked the cows twice each day. She paid the bills, and took care of her four children. And all during this time, she exchanged letters with her husband and gave him the news.

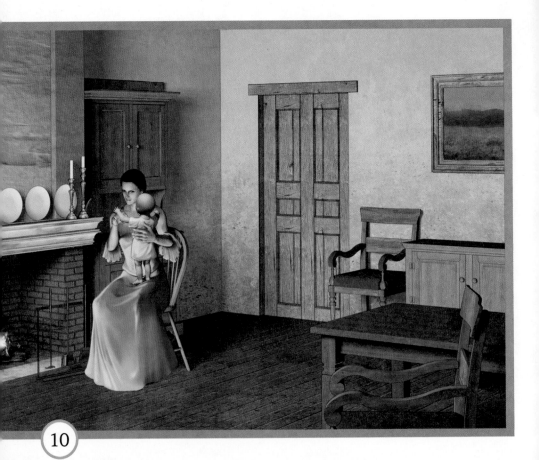

In one of her letters, Abigail Adams told how she watched a battle from a hill in Braintree.

Remember the Ladies

In her letters, Abigail Adams also gave her opinions. One of her most famous letters was dated March 31, 1776. In the letter, she asked the delegates to "remember the ladies" when they wrote new laws. She said, "Do not put such **unlimited** power into the hands of the husbands."

Speaking Out

Abigail Adams also had a strong opinion about **slavery**. She thought that slavery, which was then practiced in the colonies, was wrong. "It always appeared a most evil scheme to me," she wrote.

Serving the Country

In July 1776, Congress declared the United States an independent country. Later, Congress sent John Adams to France. Once again Abigail Adams stayed home to manage the farm.

The American Revolution finally ended in 1783. America won its independence.

John Adams continued to serve his country. He was elected the first vice president in 1788, serving with President George Washington. Then in 1796, he was elected president himself. Abigail Adams was now first lady, the wife of the president.

In this drawing, Washington is sworn in as president. John Adams is shown at his left.

The Adamses were the first family to live in the White House. They moved in before it was finished.

Mrs. President

John Adam's letters show how much he valued his wife's advice. Not everyone felt the same. People who did not like the Adamses called her "Mrs. President." They thought the president listened to his wife too much. But Abigail Adams saw no reason to stop advising her husband.

Home at Last

After John Adams's time as president ended, the couple returned to their farm. They spent seventeen more years together. Abigail Adams continued to write many letters. Today she is remembered for her strong opinions about women's rights. She is remembered for how she used her mind and how she helped her husband shape the history of our country.

Glossary

colony a place ruled by another country

delegate a person chosen to speak for others

independence freedom from another country's rule

influence the ability to have an effect on others

slavery the practice of forcing people to work without pay and without freedom

unlimited without end